Let's Explore DINOSAURS

FUN KITS

Written by Rupert Matthews

TOP THAT! Kids™

Copyright © 2004 Top That! Publishing plc
Top That! Publishing, 27023 McBean Parkway,
408 Valencia, CA 91355
Top That! Kids is a Trademark of
Top That! Publishing plc
All rights reserved
www.topthatpublishing.com

What is a Dinosaur?

Dinosaurs (dine-oh-saws) were reptiles which lived on Earth millions of years ago.

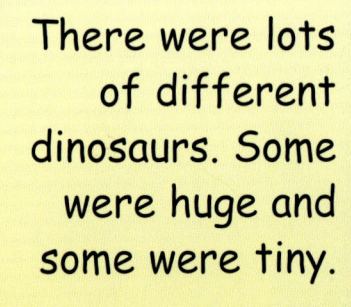

There were lots of different dinosaurs. Some were huge and some were tiny.

When did they Live?
Dinosaurs lived in the Mesozoic Era. It is divided into three periods: the Triassic (try-ass-ik) Period, the Jurassic (jurr-ass-ik) Period and the Cretaceous (kree-tay-shoos) Period.

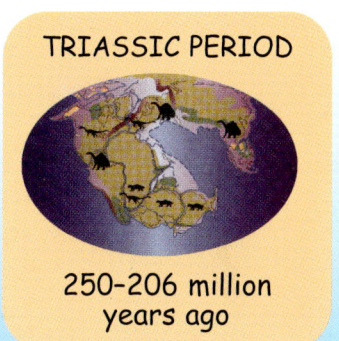

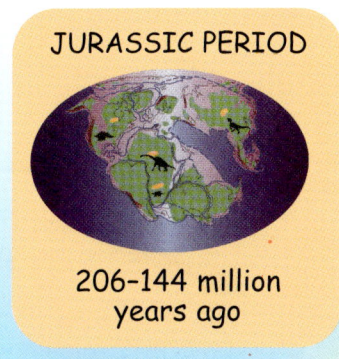

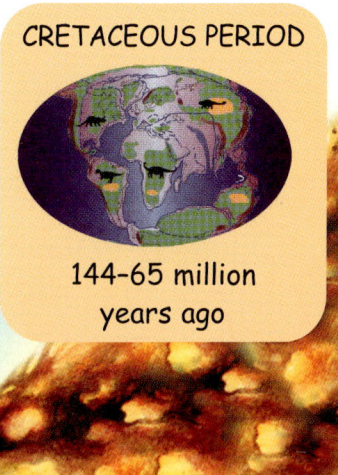

TRIASSIC PERIOD
250-206 million years ago

JURASSIC PERIOD
206-144 million years ago

CRETACEOUS PERIOD
144-65 million years ago

Where are they Now?
About 65 million years ago all the dinosaurs became extinct (died). Some people think a change in climate killed the dinosaurs. Other people think a giant asteroid hit Earth.

Dinosaur Detection

When a dinosaur died, its bones and teeth may have been buried in mud or sand. After millions of years they become fossils, which means they turned to stone.

Searching for Clues

Scientists called paleontologists (pale-ee-onn-toll-oh-jists) study dinosaur fossils. They find them in rocks and keep them in museums.

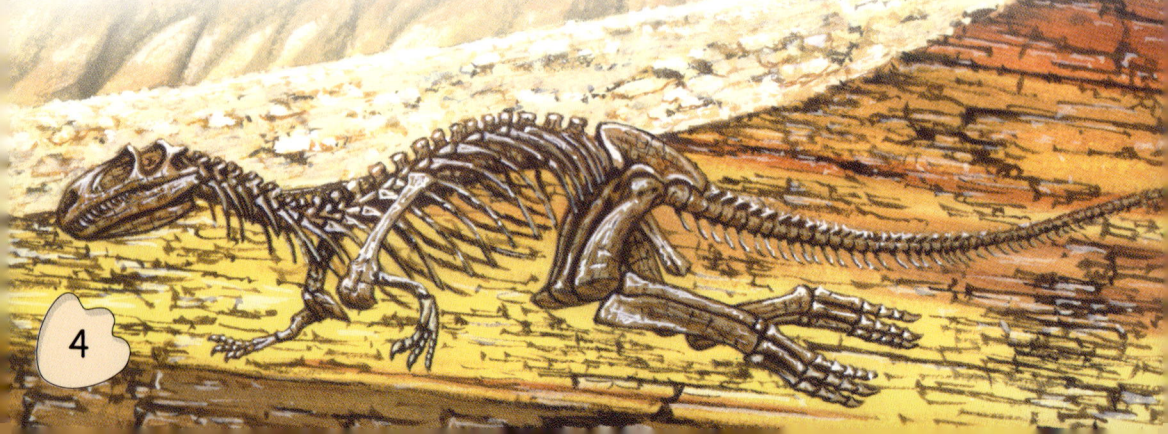

Museums
At the museum a paleontologist puts the bones back together to find out what the dinosaur looked like when it was alive.

Fossil Fun
Fossils have been found of other plants and animals. Scientists study these to find out what else lived with the dinosaurs.

5

Model Making

You need an adult to help you make your model.

1 Ask an adult for an old jug. Carefully measure 8½ fl. oz of cold water into the jug.

You will need:
four molds (from the kit)
bag of plaster (from the kit)
8½ fl. oz water
a jug and spoon

2 Pour all of the plaster into the water. Stir the mixture until it is smooth.

SAFETY RULES
Do not place the material in the mouth. Do not inhale dust or powder. Do not apply to the body. Keep younger children under the specified age limit and animals away from the activity area. Store chemical toys out of the reach of young children. Wash hands after carrying out activities. Clean all equipment which has not been supplied with the set or recommended in the instructions for use. Do not eat, drink, or smoke in the activity area.

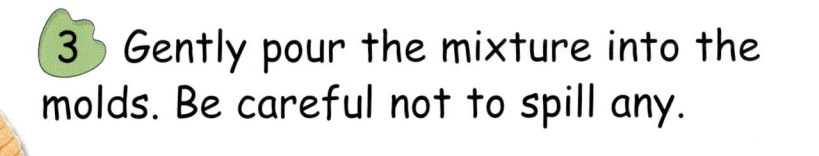

3️⃣ Gently pour the mixture into the molds. Be careful not to spill any.

4️⃣ Leave them to dry. Do not touch them for at least five hours, even if they look dry.

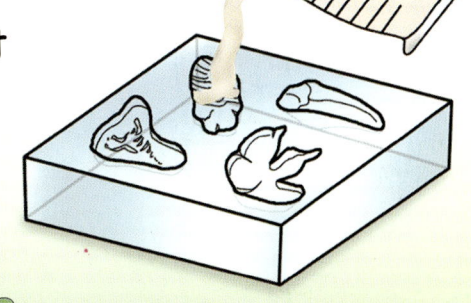

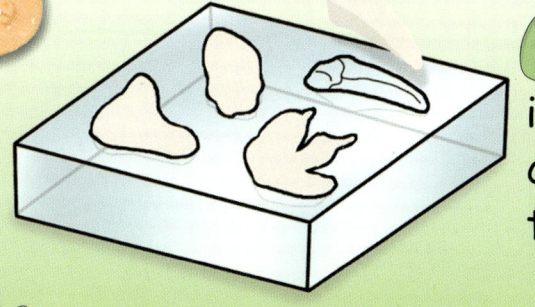

5️⃣ When the plaster is hard and dry, carefully remove from the mold.

6️⃣ Now you can paint the dinosaur models. You may be able to buy more plaster from an art store to make more models.

Dinosaur Snap

You can use the cards with this book to play an exciting game of Dinosaur Snap. You can play the game with two, three or four players.

1 Place the cards together in a pile. Carefully shuffle the cards so that they are all mixed up.

2 Deal the cards so that each player has the same number of cards. Each player holds their pile of cards face down so that they cannot see the cards.

3 The player to the left of the dealer is the first to lay a card. They take a card from the top of their pile and place it face up in the middle.

4 The player to the left of the first player then lays a card from the top of their pile on top of the card on the table.

5 Players take it in turns to lay cards until a card is laid that is the same dinosaur as the one just laid. This is a snap.

6 The first player to shout "SNAP!" wins the cards in the middle. They place them at the bottom of their pile.

7 The player who has won the snap now lays a card as before.

8 If a player runs out of cards, they are out of the game.

9 Play continues until one person has won all the cards. They are the winner of the game.

Theropods

The theropods (theer-roh-podds) were fierce and ate other creatures. Their name means "beast-foot."

Compsognathus (komp-sogg-nay-thus)
Compsognathus was the smallest dinosaur of all. It was just 24 in. long. Compsognathus ate insects and lizards.

Coelophysis
(see-low-fye-sis)
Coelophysis had long slim legs and three toes with sharp claws at the end of them.

12

Allosaurus (al-oh-saw-rus)
The name allosaurus means "different reptile." Its back bones (vertebrae) were different from those on similar dinosaurs.

Velociraptor (vee-loss-ee-rapp-torr)
Velociraptors could run very quickly to hunt other dinosaurs. They had large, curved claws on their hind legs.

Sauropods

Sauropods (saw-roh-podds) were the biggest animals ever to walk on land. All sauropods ate plants. They had long necks to reach food.

Diplodocus (dipp-loh-doh-kus) Diplodocus lived in North America during the Jurassic Period. This dinosaur grew to be 30 yards long.

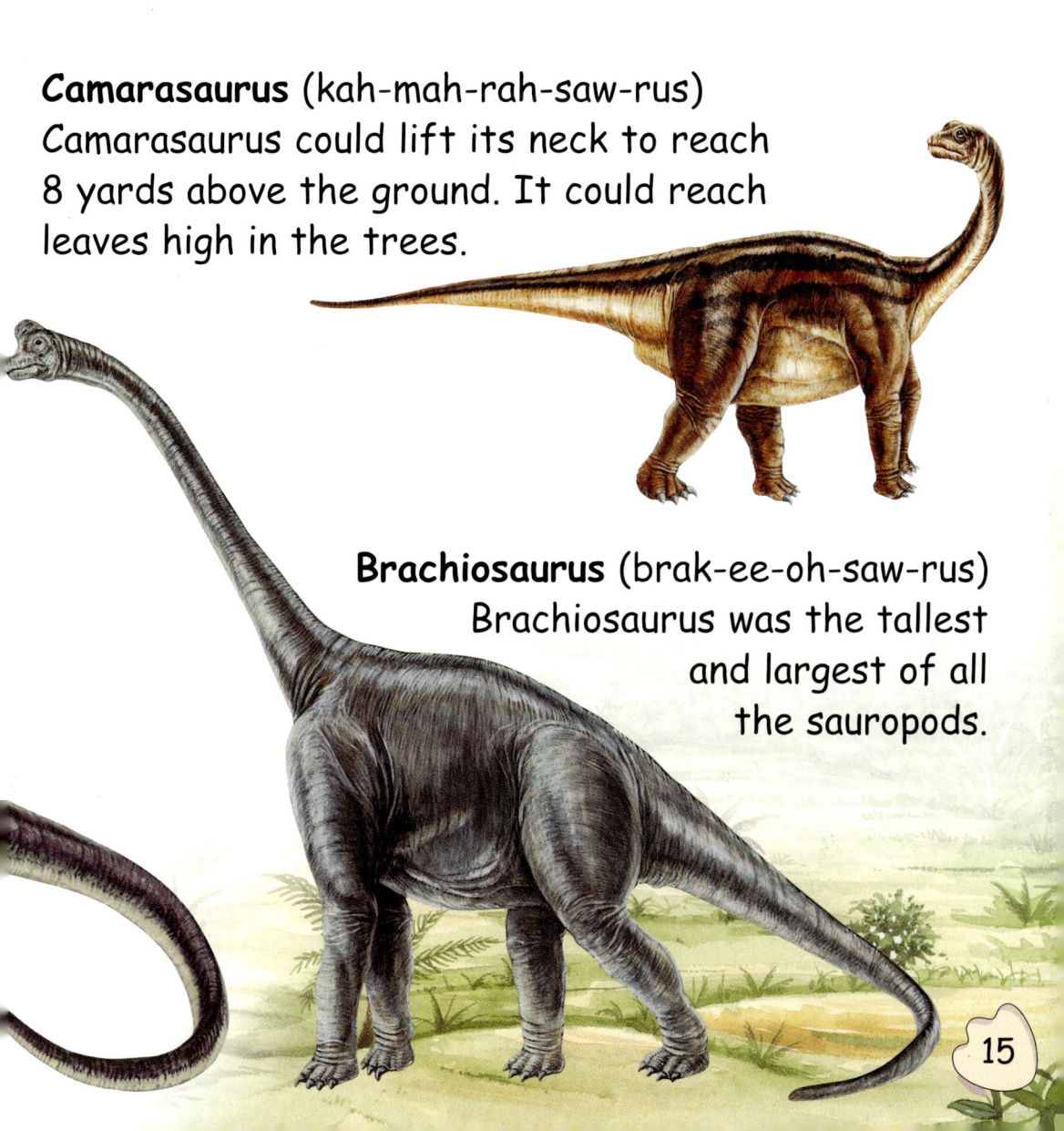

Camarasaurus (kah-mah-rah-saw-rus)
Camarasaurus could lift its neck to reach 8 yards above the ground. It could reach leaves high in the trees.

Brachiosaurus (brak-ee-oh-saw-rus)
Brachiosaurus was the tallest and largest of all the sauropods.

15

Ankylosaurs

Ankylosaurs (ann-kill-oh-saws) were plant-eating dinosaurs. They had very strong armor made of bone. Ankylosaurs lived during the Cretaceous Period.

Ankylosaurus (ann-kill-oh-saw-rus) This dinosaur had a large club of bone on the end of its tail. Even its eyelids were bony!

Polacanthus (pole-ah-kan-thus) Polacanthus had giant bone spikes for extra defense. It lived in Britain about 125 million years ago.

Euoplocephalus (yuo-plo-sef-allus)
Euoplocephalus had a bony club at the end of its tail which it used to defend itself.

Defense
If an ankylosaur was attacked by a hunting dinosaur, it may have used the bony club as a weapon.

17

Ceratopsians

The ceratopsians (serr-rah-tope-see-anns) had horns growing from their heads. Ceratopsians were found only in North America and in eastern Asia.

Torosaurus (toh-roe-saw-rus) Torosaurus had the largest skull of any land animal that ever lived. The skull was over 2½ yards long.

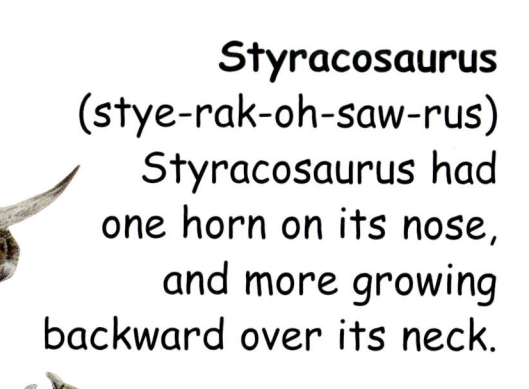

Styracosaurus
(stye-rak-oh-saw-rus)
Styracosaurus had one horn on its nose, and more growing backward over its neck.

Centrosaurus
(senn-trow-saw-rus)
Centrosaurus had one large horn. It lived in North America 75 million years ago.

Defense
Ceratopsians lived in small groups. The adults would form a ring to protect the young.

Ornithopods

Ornithopods (aw-nith-oh-podds) were plant-eating dinosaurs. Their name means "bird-foot," because they left footprints which looked like those of giant birds.

Lesothosaurus (ler-so-toe-saw-rus)
Lesothosaurus was one of the first dinosaurs. It lived about 215 million years ago in South Africa. Lesothosaurus was about 28 in. long.

Lambeosaurus (lamm-bee-oh-saw-rus)
This dinosaur had a large crest of bone pointing forward on its head. The crest may have been brightly colored.

Maiasaura (mye-ah-saw-rah)
Scientists have found fossils of Maiasaura eggs and babies. The dinosaurs laid eggs in round nests. The adults fed and cared for the young.

Parasaurolophus (pah-rah-saw-roh-loh-fus)
This dinosaur had a long crest of bone on top of its head. Air tubes inside the crest formed part of the nose. Perhaps Parasaurolophus used the tubes to call very loudly to other dinosaurs.

Pachycephalosaurs

Pachycephalosaurs (pack-ee-keff-ah-loh-saws) were among the very last dinosaurs on Earth. They lived about 65 million years ago in Asia and North America. The name Pachycephalosaur means "thick-head-reptile."

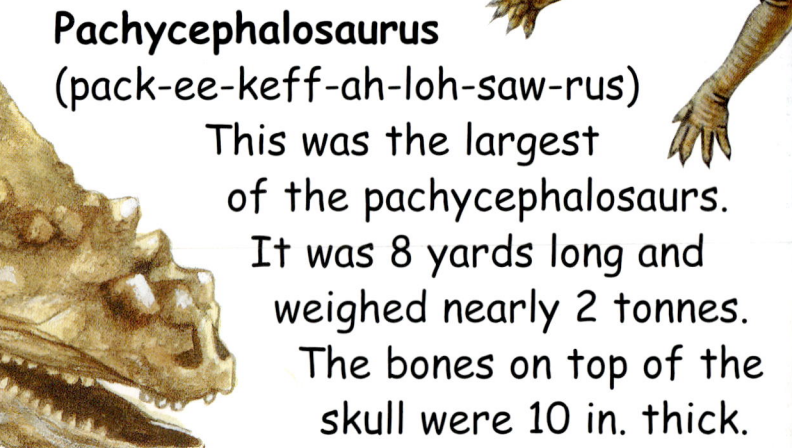

Pachycephalosaurus (pack-ee-keff-ah-loh-saw-rus) This was the largest of the pachycephalosaurs. It was 8 yards long and weighed nearly 2 tonnes. The bones on top of the skull were 10 in. thick.

Headbangers
Pachycephalosaurs may have hit their thick heads together when fighting. The winner of the fight would have led the herd.

Mountain Dinosaurs
Paleontologists think that the pachycephalosaurs lived among the mountains. They may have looked for plants to eat among the rocks.

Stegosaurs

Stegosaurs (stegg-oh-saws) were plant-eating dinosaurs. They walked on all four legs. These dinosaurs had plates and spikes of bone growing out of their backs and along their tails.

Jurassic Dinosaurs

Most stegosaurs lived between 170 and 130 million years ago during the Jurassic Period.

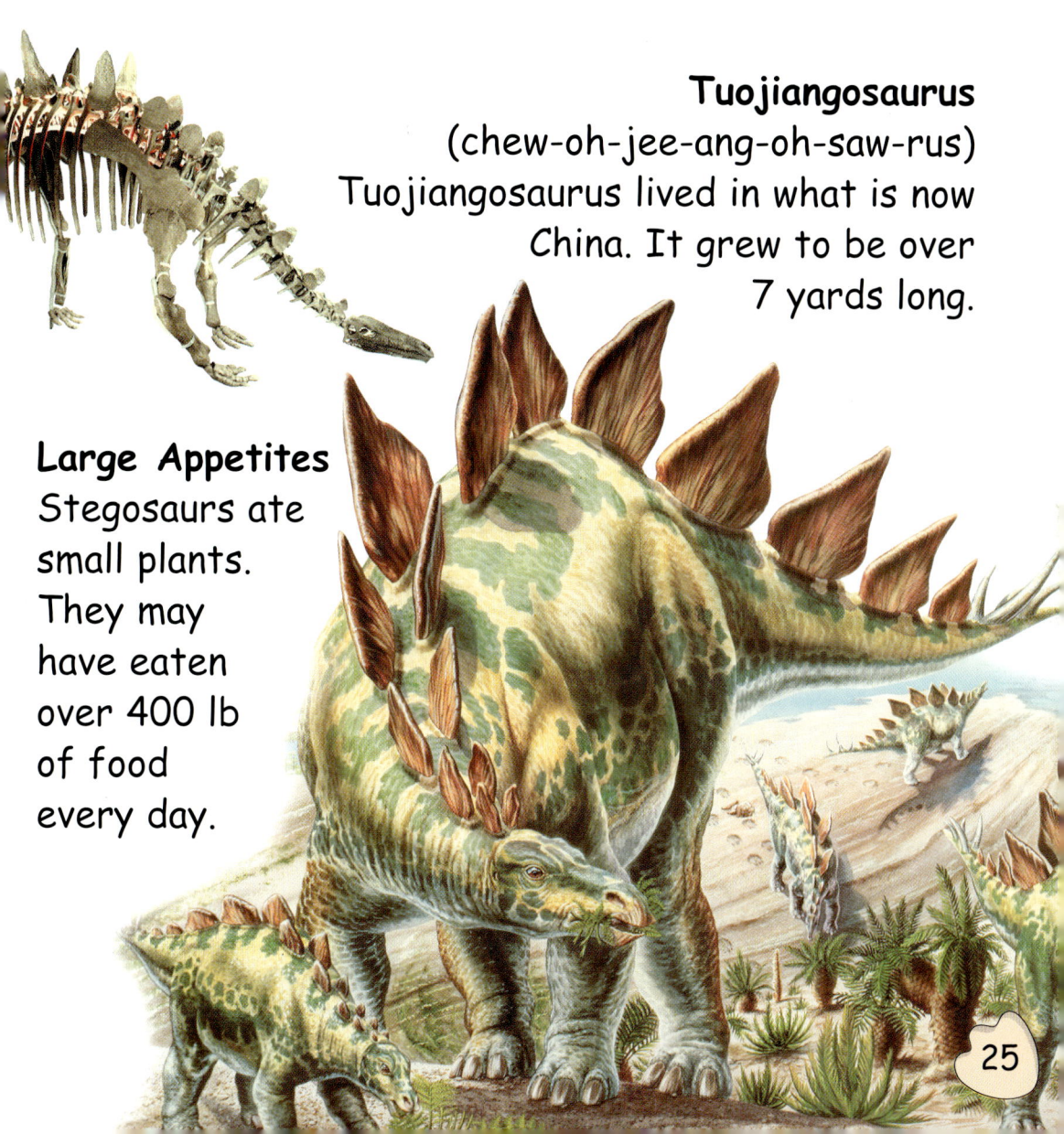

Tuojiangosaurus
(chew-oh-jee-ang-oh-saw-rus)
Tuojiangosaurus lived in what is now China. It grew to be over 7 yards long.

Large Appetites
Stegosaurs ate small plants. They may have eaten over 400 lb of food every day.

Coelophysis

Coelophysis (see-low-fye-sis) was a small type of theropod dinosaur. It lived about 215 million years ago in North America. Coelophysis was one of the very first dinosaurs.

Features
Coelophysis had a long neck and many sharp teeth. The head could move quickly, so Coelophysis could snap up food.

Hunter
Coelophysis ate small animals such as lizards, newts and insects.

Finger Food
The front legs of Coelophysis ended with three strong fingers. These were used to hold food.

Allosaurus

Allosaurus (al-oh-saw-rus) was a large theropod dinosaur. It grew to be 14 yards long and ate other large dinosaurs.

Colorful Crests

The head of Allosaurus had two crests of bone running along it. These might have been brightly colored so that Allosaurus could recognize each other.

Sharp Teeth

Allosaurus teeth were very sharp and curved backward. This meant they could bite deep into other animals.

Tyrannosaurus Rex

Tyrannosaurus rex (tie-rann-oh-saw-rus recks) was a powerful hunter. Its name means "king of the tyrant reptiles."

Giant Jaws
The jaws of Tyrannosaurus were three times as powerful as those of a modern lion.

Big Foot
The hind feet were large and wide. They may have helped the dinosaur move quietly when hunting.

Balancing Act
The tail of Tyrannosaurus was long and heavy to help it balance.

How to Make Your Dinosaur Skeleton

Just follow these steps to complete your amazing dinosaur skeleton. When instructions refer to the left or right of the dinosaur, you should assume that it is facing you. The pieces are put together in numbered order starting with number 1, followed by number 2 and so on...

1 Take the right leg and push slot 1 into slot 1 on the leg support piece. Take the left leg and push slot 2 into slot 2 on the other leg support piece.

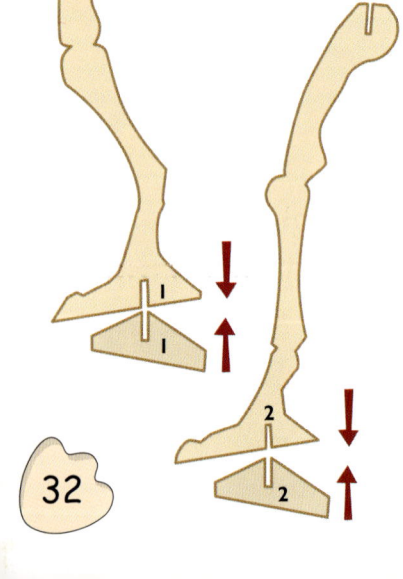

32

2 Now carefully push the legs, together with their support pieces, firmly into the base as shown in the picture. To join the legs together, take the hip connector and push slot 5 into slot 5 on the right leg. Slot 6 pushes down into slot 6 on the left leg.

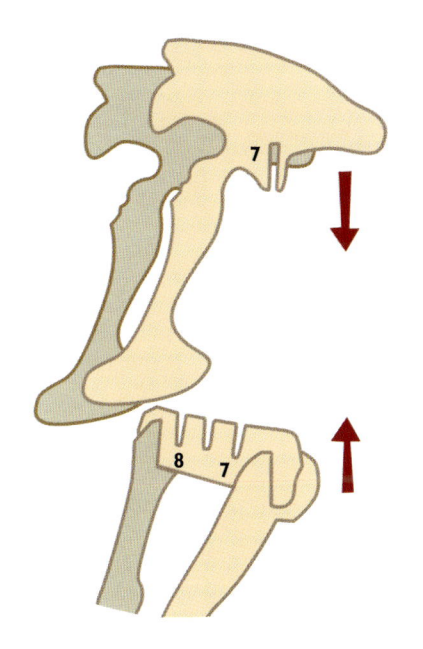

3 Next come the pelvis bones. Take the right pelvis and push slot 7 into slot 7 on the hip connector. Then push slot 8 on the left pelvis into slot 8 on the hip connector.

33

4 Take the spine piece and push slot 9 down into slot 9 on the hip connector.

5 To make the dinosaur's tail, take the tail piece and the tail connector and put them together by sliding slot 10 on the tail into slot 10 on the tail connector. Make sure the sides are pressed into the two slots towards the end of the tail to secure it firmly. The tail now connects to the body by pushing slot 11 on the tail into slot 11 on the spine.

34

6 Now for the front end of the dinosaur. Take the neck piece and push it downward into the slot numbered 12 to secure it in place.

7 Now for the ribs. Start at the front of the neck and push the first rib in place by slotting down number 13 into slot 13 on the neck. Continue backward toward the tail by pushing all the ribs numbered 14 to 23 down into their slots on the neck.

8 Take the head connector and push slot 24 into slot 24 on the neck piece.

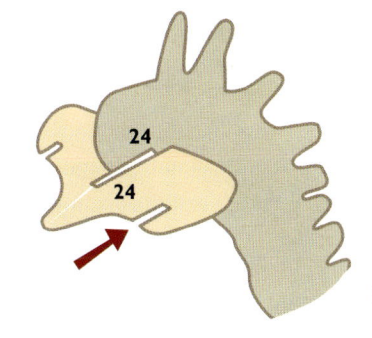

35

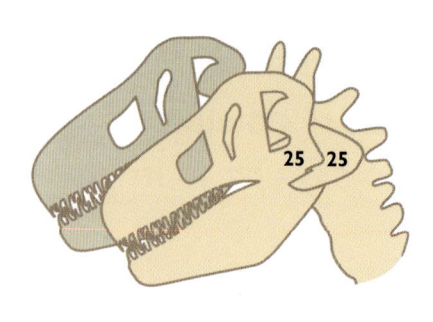

9 For the dinosaur's head, take the right head piece and push slot 25 into slot 25 on the head connector. Then take the left head piece and push slot 26 into slot 26 on the head connector.

10 Add the shoulders by pushing slot 27 on the right shoulder into slot 27 on the arm connector. Then push slot 28 on the left shoulder into slot 28 on the arm connector.

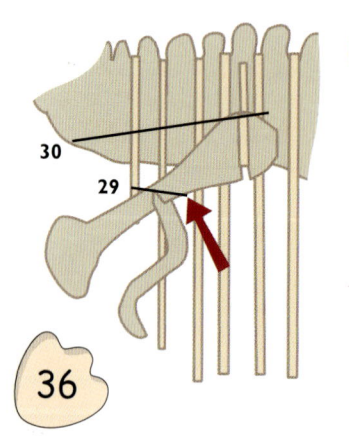

11 Add the arms by pushing them upward onto the shoulders. Slot 29 on the right arm goes onto the small marker numbered 29 on the right shoulder and slot 30 on the left arm goes onto the marker numbered 30 on the left shoulder. Bend the shoulders slightly to face inward.

12 Take the neck connector and push slot 31 into slot 31 on the neck.

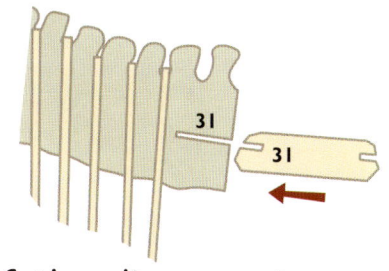

13 To add the front half of the dinosaur to the back half simply push them together with slots numbered 32 on the spine and neck connector interlocking.

14 To complete your dinosaur, push the tail support piece into the tiny link piece, making sure that slot 33 goes onto the small marker on the tiny link piece numbered 33. Slot 34 on the link piece goes over the marker numbered 34 on the spine.

37

Giganotosaurus

Giganotosaurus (jig-a-not-oh-saw-rus) was the largest meat-eating animal ever to walk on land. It was over 14 yards long and weighed about 8 tonnes.

Cretaceous Dinosaur
Giganotosaurus lived in South America about 95 million years ago, during the Cretaceous Period.

Scissor-Teeth
This dinosaur had a skull 2 yards long. Its teeth worked like a pair of scissors to cut through food.

Iguanodon

Iguanodon (ig-wah-no-don) lived in Europe about 100 million years ago during the Cretaceous Period.

Thumb Spike
Iguanodon had a large, sharp spike on its thumb. It may have used this to fight off hunting dinosaurs.

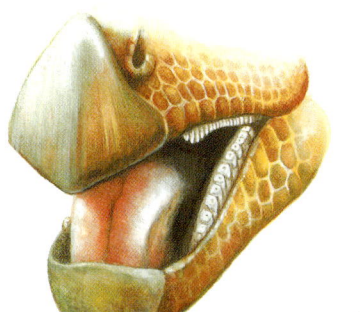

What a Mouthful
Iguanodon had over 100 teeth to help it grind up tough plants.

First Fossils
Iguanodon was one of the first dinosaurs to be discovered. The fossils were found by Dr Gideon Mantell in Britain in 1822.

Brachiosaurus

Brachiosaurus (brak-ee-oh-saw-rus) was one of the heaviest dinosaurs. It weighed over 85 tonnes, the same as thirteen elephants.

Long Legs
Brachiosaurus was the only dinosaur which had front legs longer than its hind legs.

Food Finder
Brachiosaurus had a claw on its front foot. It may have used the claw to dig for food.

Smells Tasty
It may have used the large nostrils on top of its head to find out if food was good to eat.

Stegosaurus

Stegosaurus (stegg-oh-saw-rus) was the largest of the stegosaur dinosaurs. It was 9 yards long.

Bony Plates
The large plates along its back may have been brightly colored to signal to other Stegosaurus.

Scary Spikes
The long spikes on the end of the tail could be swung from side to side to frighten off hunting dinosaurs.

Neck Covering
The neck of Stegosaurus was protected by hundreds of tiny pieces of bone.

Triceratops

Triceratops (try-serr-ah-tops) was a ceratopsian dinosaur. It lived in North America about 65 million years ago.

Late Dinosaur
Triceratops was one of the very last dinosaurs. After Triceratops there were no dinosaurs living anywhere on Earth.

Beak
Triceratops had a beak like a parrot's. It used the beak to bite leaves off plants.

47

Dinosaurs Today

The last dinosaur died about 65 million years ago.

Finding Out
You can visit a museum to look at fossils and learn more about dinosaurs.

Still Alive Today
Some creatures on Earth are related to dinosaurs. Scientists believe that crocodiles, sharks, and even birds have come from dinosaurs.